My First Sinhala Words for Communication

Picture Book with English Translations

Published By: My First Picture Book™

A Heartfelt Message from Our Publishers:

Your support does more than just buy a book. It uplifts native authors and fuels the dreams of a close-knit business. We value every reader, and your insights could shape our next bestseller! Got suggestions or feedback? Let's co-create magic. Connect with us through the 'Contact Us' section on our website at **MyFirstPictureBook.com**.

Accident

අනතුර

ana-thu-ra

Come

එන්න

en-na

Fire

ගිනි

gi-ni

Food

ආහාර

aa-ha-ra

Go

යන්න

yan-na

Hello

ආයුබෝවන්

a-yu-bo-wan

Help

උදව්

uda-wu

Maybe

සමහර විට

sa-ma-ha-ra vi-ta

Medicine

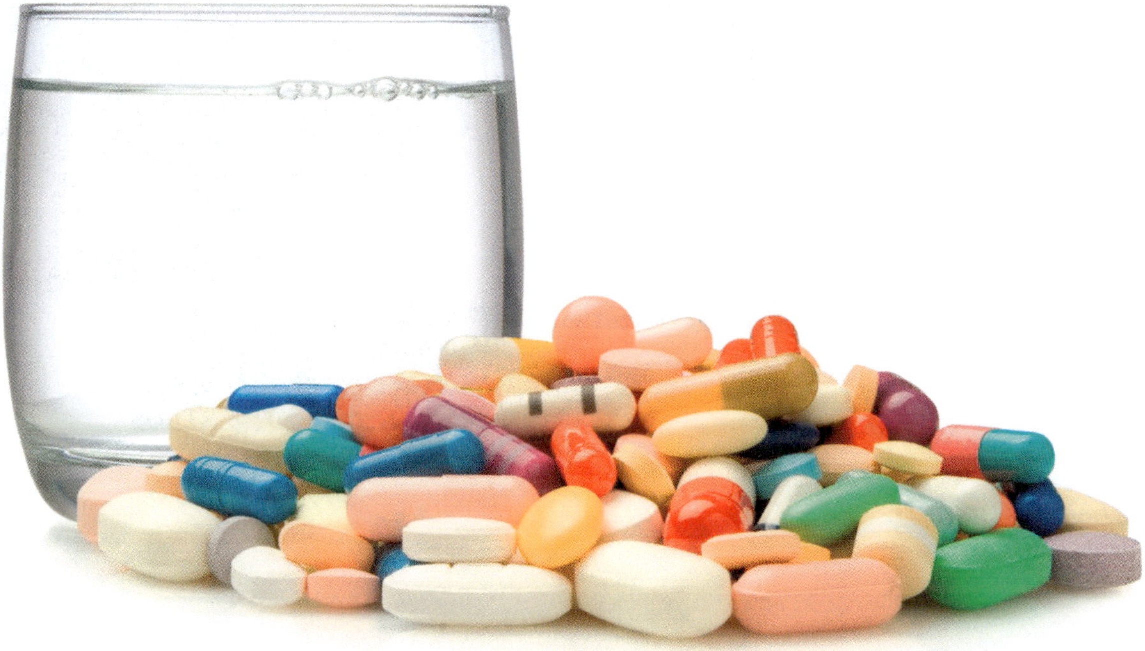

ඖෂධය

aush-dha-ya

Nothing

කිසිවක් නැත

ki-si-wak nae-tha

Ok

හරි

ha-ri

Please

කරුණාකර

ka-ru-naa-ka-ra

Police

පොලීසිය

po-lee-si-ya

Price

මිල

mi-la

Pull

අදින්න

a-din-na

Push

තල්ලු කරන්න

thal-lu ka-ran-na

Slow

මන්දගාමී

man-da-gaa-mi

Soon

ඉක්මනින්

ik-ma-nin

Sorry

සමාවන්න

sa-maa-wan-na

Thank You

ඔයාට ස්තූතියි

o-yaa-ta stu-thi-yi

Thief

හොරා

ho-raa

Wait

ඉන්න

in-na

What?

කුමක් ද?

ku-mak-da

When?

කවදා ද?

ka-wa-daa da

Where?

කොහෙද?

ko-he-da

Who?

කවුද?

ka-wu-da

Why?

ඇයි?

ae-yi

Yes

ඔව්

ow

No

නැහැ

nae-hae

Up

ඉහළට

i-ha-la-ta

Down

පහළට

pa-ha-la-ta

Left

වමට

wa-ma-ta

Right

දකුණට

da-ku-na-ta

North

උතුරු

u-thu-ru

South

දකුණු

da-ku-nu

East

නැගෙනහිර

nae-ge-na-hi-ra

West

බටහිර

ba-ta-hi-ra

Printed in Great Britain
by Amazon

50603222R00023